The Circle Of Life.

Stacey Smith

BookLeaf Publishing

India | USA | UK

Presentation by *BookLeaf Publishing*

Web: www.bookleafpub.com

E-mail: info@bookleafpub.com

ISBN : 9789357447478

First edition 2021

DEDICATION

For Marco. The one constant in my life who never stopped believing in me, who reminds me everyday without fail that he loves me, and who reassures me that despite my crazy, I am a good Mum.

Writing these poems has been a difficult process as it's forced me to open wounds that had been plastered over and, as a result, it's put me in a dark place a few times. Without Marco's love and constant support, I would not have been able to complete this book.

So to you Marco, my beautiful handsome son, I dedicate this book. xxx

Reinterpreted

So how do I breath with this weight on my chest
The tightening and heaviness it's creating within.
Wrestling and writhing, beckoning for less
From the constant endless pain I'm in.
I beg, plead and please don't stay
Heal the wounds that this pain spawns
Damage forged in the darkness of day
Begging for relief that never comes.
Suffocating burden some do yearn
Boasting the Importance of nature's ways
Never content till afflictions firm
Then questions of mental stability cascades
So how do I breath with this weight on my chest
The tightening and heaviness it's creating within
Wrestling and writhing beckoning for less
From the constant endless pain I'm in.

Endless Pain

Flutter like a butterfly
And you make me cry
Envisioning you
what can I do?
My feelings are strong
Don't tell me I'm wrong
Do you feel the same
Or are my feelings in vain
Leave me alone and let me be
I don't want the kindness you're giving to me
Love me instead and give me your vows
Making my heart beat out of my blouse
Will you ever see
How happy we could be
Our love intertwined
In heart and in mind
You touched my soul
And fulfilled your role
And I'd do the same
Without any shame
Delusional obsessive
I'm just expressive
But I see potential
For love that's essential
You finessed my mind

And now I'm blind
For in love's world
My senses curled
To your scent
My life is spent
And all that's left
Is a victim of theft
You robbed my love
Like a thief from above
Imprisoned and chained
My life is drained.
So leave me be
Please set me free
To where I belong
In a lonely song
Free from pain
Embarrassing shame
Untamed and wild
A vulnerable child

Vulnerable Child

Oh sweet baby come and take my hand
Let me remind you what love feels like
How it should be and not how they think
Wrap my arms around you and feel my warmth
Broken may isolate and hide you away
But I got you, I do, I promise, have faith.

Oh sweet child I know it's lonely where you are
Stop chasing after broken, broken can't fix you.
Exposure to the world left you damaged and
weak
You sought comfort, love and safety I know.
You give yourself freely thinking you'll get more
in return.
But I got you, have faith, I do, I know

Oh sweet girl, don't loose who you are.
You're an intelligent being with a beautiful light
Illuminating every dark path that you walk
Don't chase after broken please don't go
It's not worth the pain, you'll loose yourself.
You can't fix what broken wants to keep
Stand tall and proud and stand your ground.

Oh sweet young lady look at you now,

You broke and mended scars on your soul
Where is broken? You don't know?
But you carry on as each day is a new.
You fall, you cry, you're aching still
For love, comfort and warmth
It's okay, it's okay, I know, it's okay
You're getting there, keep holding on
To the thoughts of strength, love and faith.
Loosen my hand now, broken is gone
Let go of the protection of my arms
You have love, strength and warmth
You got you!

Oh vulnerable child, what a life we've had
It took a while but our story continues.
So take a deep breath and hold your head high
For today is a another day
You'll face with a smile.

Face with a smile.

Faces with a smile
Laugh with the joy of a child
Be untamed and wild.

Faces with a smile
Wails don't belong to the mild
Be untamed and wild.

Faces with a smile
Be happy in all your trials
Too, untamed and wild.

Faces with a smile
Content and happy a while
Be untamed and wild.

Untamed and wild

Untamed and wild
Never conforming
To the world's notion of acceptance
Aesthetically designed to
Mirror the beauty of
Every wild animal
Depicting freedom

Achieving the impossible with
Nirvana rising
Dissolving hoplessness

Wander through the forests night
Ignoring the pain of the past
Living in the here and now
Diffusing pain and rejection

Pain and rejection

You know how it goes
That feeling, when it shows
Gains momentum, never slows
And the pain inside just grows
Like a ball of air that flows
Along nerve paths you can not close
And the feeling is exposed
But never once opposed
All you can do is hold
Yourself as if you're cold
My tears a story told
Rejection is my mould
If my heart were to unfold
You'd see cracks and scars that's old
Abandoned, unconsoled
Married to a grief bestowed;
Arranged and now I know
That there's no help or a hero
Dark nights I'm lonely low
And so I hug my cold pillow
Silent cries that never show
The pain my heart will always grow
This empty feeling deep below
I don't know where to go.
So discard this reject bride

With the trash, and cast aside
A reject magnet guide
And any hope of love denied.
I'll take this heart and hide
It's less of eight ounces and pride
I'll rebuild the heart from deep inside
And promise a love I'll provide.

A love I'll provide

Warm to the touch
Never far away
You'll never worry much
And I will never stray
I pinkey finger swear
If you lose your way
I'll find you so don't fear
You will be okay.
We'll dance by the fire
I'll hold you close to me
Anything that you desire
Is yours eternally.
I'll encourage you 'pursue your dreams
You're capable of anything'
The world is tearing at it's seams
But happiness is what you bring.

We'll dance and sing in the rain
Taking pictures all day long
Folks will think we've gone insane
As we sing our favourite song.
We'll talk until the sun can't stay
As the moon starts it's ascent,
All that life has thrown our way
But yet we're still content.

Some things may upset you
You may not always know why
But with me here I'll get you through
Cause' You're my baby boy.
We'll laugh away the tears
And I'll hold you up strong
I'll help you scare away your fears
Cause' with us they don't belong.

So continue on growing
In the fashion that you are
And I promise you one simple thing,
You will go far.
Stubborn, loving, full of wit
Ambitious, that also
Don't you change one little bit
As I watch you grow.

As I watch you grow

Two little hands
Two little feet
Two and a heartbeat
Who will you take after
Me or your dad
A brand new chapter
That's waiting to be had
I feel you move
I feel you grow
My love is proved
To you I'll show

You're here, you're here
Yes you are
I've got you my dear
In my arms
A head full of hair
And pouty little lips
Everyone's here
To see your little hands - grips
My little finger

Don't you let it go
They can wait a little longer
Whilst I shower you with love.

Your eyes catch mine
We form a bond so strong
And in that moment, my life is fine
And nothing can go wrong
You're crawling now
You're on your way
I don't know how
Time's run away
Your hair curls down
Your sweet soft face
God I'm so proud
Of what he helped create

My title, my new name
Brings music to my ears
As we play a made up game
That will last throughout the years
You giggle, laugh and scream
As I catch you while you run
And on my face, a smile beams
When you think the game you've won.
I tuck you into bed
And read your favourite story
You hang on every word that's said
And fall asleep before me.

Blink of an eye
Here we are
Life's passed us by
And you've come far
Your seventeen
And I'm growing old
So many things you've seen
And stories left untold.
You're handsome tall and strong
Full of wit and caring too
I'm proud to call you son
I love you, I love you.

I love you

Once there was a time
I could say I love you
Our time was sublime
And for that I loved you
You showed me life
With you in it
But never the knife
That bit you hid.

There were the days
I told you love you
I was in such a haze
When I said I loved you
I let you perform
Open heart surgery
And let you transform
Everything about me.

There were the nights
I would whisper I love you
We would dance in the lights
And I knew then I loved you
You opened me up
And I bared my soul

You then closed me up
And left a hole

Once there was a time
You never said you love me
No, it's not a crime
But I needed you to love me
You showed me life
You helped me grow
But stopped the drive
You set to go.

There never was a time
That you loved me
That truth is hard to climb
Trust me
The lies in your eyes
Bought the guise
To my demise
The lesson that's in session
Is avoidance of obsession.

Obsession

Obsession in its sweetest form
Craving all and so much more
Needing every little drop
And not knowing when to stop.
The sight and smell intoxicating
New senses are fabricated
Confessing my aggression
Needs discretion in my sessions
Unfiltered and raw
Open wounds and all
So shower me clouds
Make your daily rounds
Cleanse my addiction
And let those rain drops run.

Let those rain drops run

Darkness descends up above
Everyone prepares down below
Shutters close
Gutters open
Swarms of birds head home.
Homes get warmer
Outside's colder
Condensation
On glass windows.
A slither, a crack
They can't take no more
They burst at the seams
And let the rain run.
They all take shelter
And scream as if it burns
But I, I bask in this
Let the rain drops run,
Trickle down on my face
The cold against my skin
Refreshing, so pure
Bathe me of my sin
The winters feel

Fresh and crisp
Haze from the sun
Keep me in this place.

Keep me in this place

Perfection
Submission
Shielding
Seraphic
Paradisical
Unearthly
Gratifying
Comforting
Captivating
Enthralling
Exceptional
Enchanting

Enchanting

A look, a glance that twinkle in your eye,
That beautiful smile, that's so divine
A tilt of the head
A rub of the arm
Your every move read
When you put on the charm
Your stature and physique
Has me mesmerised
You got me feeling weak
As your shape I've memorised.
You say hello
I'm weak at the knees
Infatuation grows
Like an infectious disease.
You look and move in closer
You fill my entire view
But I question if this exposure
Is the best thing for me or you.
Silence around us ensues
As our gazes meet again
With this feeling I know I'll lose
And fall into descent
So I'll stay safe right here
In this enchanting space
And freeze our time my dear

So we're always in this place.

Always in this place

Liking the stability
Inviting a change
Moving from a stationed state
Bringing new experiences
On a brand new day

Brand new day.

It's a brand new day
Happiness beams in our hearts
Warm feelings inside

Let the day begin
With a smile and brand new lives
Senses awakened

Senses awakened

And suddenly I'm in the room
Nothing makes sense
A rebirthing of knowledge
Has flooded my mind
Artillery prepared
Every touch
Every smell
Every sound
Like chalk to the board
Salt to the wound
Lost in a maze
Nauseous
Ready for the war
But untrained
Trembling
Ears pricked to every move
I question can I handle this.
Can I do this
I can do this?
I can do this.
I sit and write a letter

...

A letter for you

A letter for you

When you close your eyes
I want you to smile
And think fondly of me
All of the time
I wasn't there for long
But that's okay
For I experienced what most never do
A lifetime of love, every minute.
I know you miss me
I miss you too
I've only ever known love
How many can say that?
You held me close
I felt your warmth
I hope you felt mine too.
You told me you loved me
And promised you always will
I hung on every word
And to this day
Believe you still.
This battle that so many of us face
Makes me know I'm not alone
You aren't alone
You never are.
I love you

My mother
My father
And sister
And I know I'm loved too
I read every letter written
And hold them close to my heart.
And wait till we meet again.
So when you close your eyes
I want you to smile
And think fondly of me
As I think fondly of you

....

. . . .

Don't think of this just finished
I've only just begun
A new world has opened up
And some battles have been won
There will be trials of every kind
Of that you can be sure
But if everyone looked deep inside
They'd find a love that's pure
Optimistic, glass half full
They label, I don't mind
If there's no positivity
Then we'll all be left behind.

So I say I'm not gone,
Only ciao for now
A hug, a kiss, a gazeful look
I say thank you, and take a bow.